B♭ TRUMPET

Sounds of Celebration

Solos with Ensemble Arrangements for Two or More Players

Arranged by Stan Pethel

CONTENTS

DIGITAL DOWNLOAD CODE
To access audio MP3 files, go to:
www.halleonard.com/mylibrary

Enter Code
2025-7328-3330-7366

I0808905

Daybreak® MUSIC
EXCLUSIVELY DISTRIBUTED BY
HAL•LEONARD

As the Deer
(with "My Faith Looks Up to Thee")

B♭ TRUMPET
Solo

Words and Music by **MARTIN NYSTROM**
Arranged by **STAN PETHEL**

As the Deer
(with "My Faith Looks Up to Thee")

B♭ TRUMPET
Ensemble

Words and Music by **MARTIN NYSTROM**
Arranged by **STAN PETHEL**

Give Thanks
(with "Now Thank We All Our God")

B♭ TRUMPET
Solo

Words and Music by **HENRY SMITH**
Arranged by **STAN PETHEL**

NOW THANK WE ALL OUR GOD
German Words by MARTIN RINKART, English Translation by CATHERINE WINKWORTH
Music by JOHANN CRÜGER

Give Thanks

(with "Now Thank We All Our God")

B♭ TRUMPET
Ensemble

Words and Music by **HENRY SMITH**
Arranged by **STAN PETHEL**

Glorify Thy Name
(with "We Will Glorify")

B♭ TRUMPET
Solo

Words and Music by **DONNA ADKINS**
Arranged by **STAN PETHEL**

Glorify Thy Name
(with "We Will Glorify")

B♭ TRUMPET
Ensemble

Words and Music by **DONNA ADKINS**
Arranged by **STAN PETHEL**

Great Is the Lord

B♭ TRUMPET
Solo

Words and Music by **MICHAEL W. SMITH**
and **DEBORAH D. SMITH**
Arranged by **STAN PETHEL**

Great Is the Lord

B♭ TRUMPET
Ensemble

Words and Music by MICHAEL W. SMITH
and DEBORAH D. SMITH
Arranged by STAN PETHEL

He Is Exalted

(with "O For a Thousand Tongues to Sing")

B♭ TRUMPET
Solo

Words and Music by **TWILA PARIS**
Arranged by **STAN PETHEL**

He Is Exalted

(with "O For a Thousand Tongues to Sing")

B♭ TRUMPET
Ensemble

Words and Music by **TWILA PARIS**
Arranged by **STAN PETHEL**

I Love You Lord

(with "My Jesus, I Love Thee")

B♭ TRUMPET
Solo

Words and Music by **LAURIE KLEIN**
Arranged by **STAN PETHEL**

I Love You Lord

(with "My Jesus, I Love Thee")

B♭ TRUMPET
Ensemble

Words and Music by **LAURIE KLEIN**
Arranged by **STAN PETHEL**

Lord, I Lift Your Name on High
(with "All Hail the Power of Jesus' Name")

B♭ TRUMPET
Solo

Words and Music by **RICK FOUNDS**
Arranged by **STAN PETHEL**

B♭ Trumpet solo

Lord, I Lift Your Name on High

(with "All Hail the Power of Jesus' Name")

B♭ TRUMPET
Ensemble

Words and Music by **RICK FOUNDS**
Arranged by **STAN PETHEL**

B♭ Trumpet ensemble

More Precious than Silver

(with "When I Survey the Wondrous Cross")

B♭ TRUMPET
Solo

Words and Music by **LYNN DESHAZO**
Arranged by **STAN PETHEL**

Not too fast, with expression (♩ = *ca.* 108)

More Precious than Silver
(with "When I Survey the Wondrous Cross")

B♭ TRUMPET
Ensemble

Words and Music by **LYNN DESHAZO**
Arranged by **STAN PETHEL**

Shine, Jesus, Shine

Words and Music by **GRAHAM KENDRICK**
Arranged by **STAN PETHEL**

B♭ TRUMPET
Solo

Shine, Jesus, Shine

B♭ TRUMPET
Ensemble

Words and Music by **GRAHAM KENDRICK**
Arranged by **STAN PETHEL**

Shout to the Lord

B♭ TRUMPET
Solo

Words and Music by **DARLENE ZSCHECH**
Arranged by **STAN PETHEL**

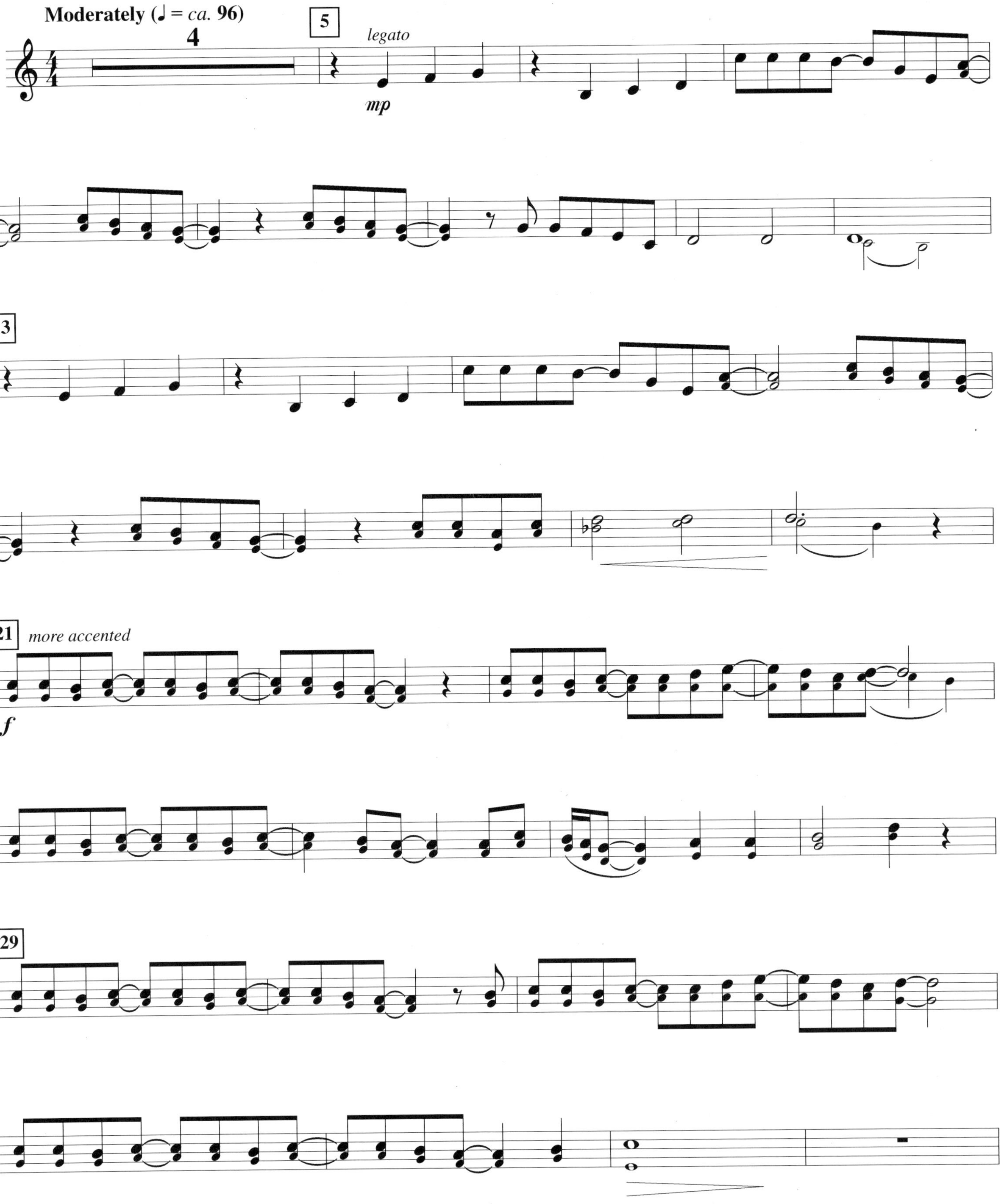

37
legato
mp
42
45
47
51
53
more accented
f
55
59
61
63
67
71
ff
rit.

Shout to the Lord

B♭ TRUMPET
Ensemble

Words and Music by **DARLENE ZSCHECH**
Arranged by **STAN PETHEL**